Fashion Drawing Games

Drawing Book for Girls

Speedy Kids

SPEEDY KIDS
Children's Fiction

Use the grid to copy the image.

Can you draw this?

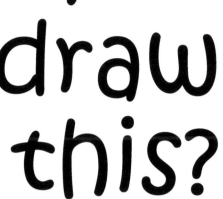

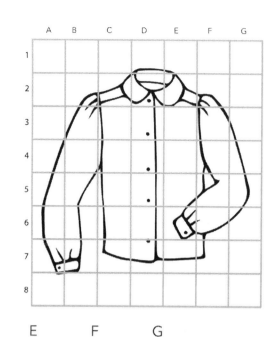

	A	B	C	D	E	F	G
1							
2							
3							
4							
5							
6							
7							
8							

Can you draw this?

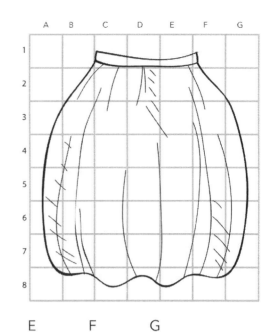

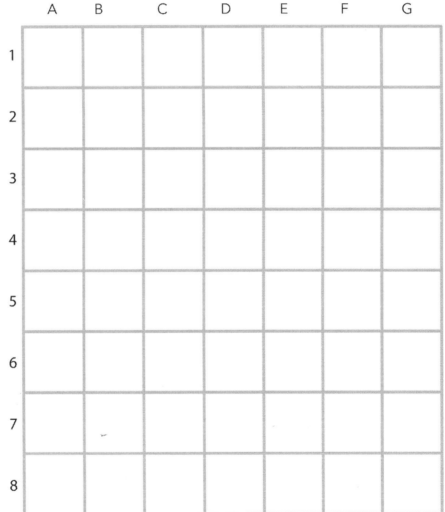

Can you draw this?

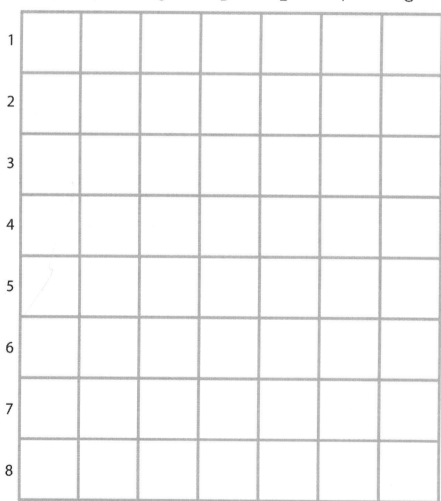

Can you draw this?

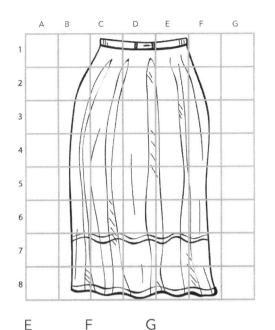

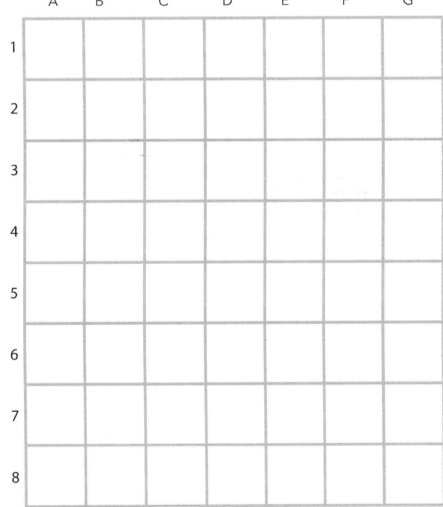

Can you draw this?

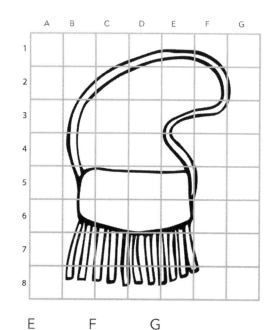

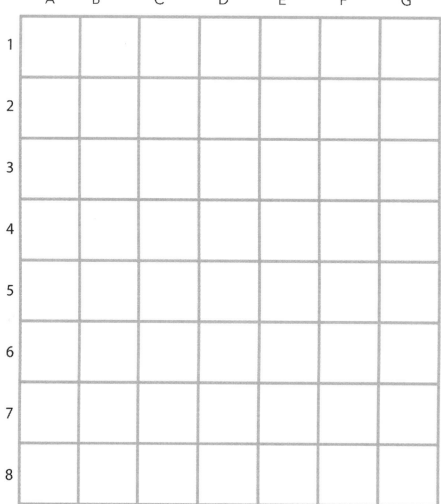

Can you draw this?

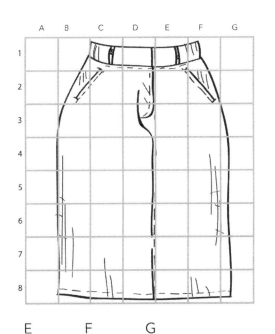

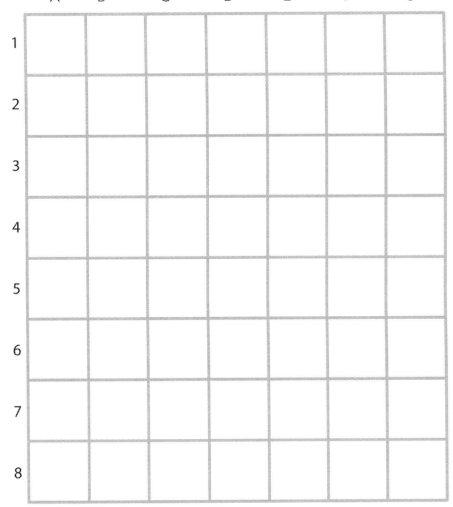

Can you draw this?

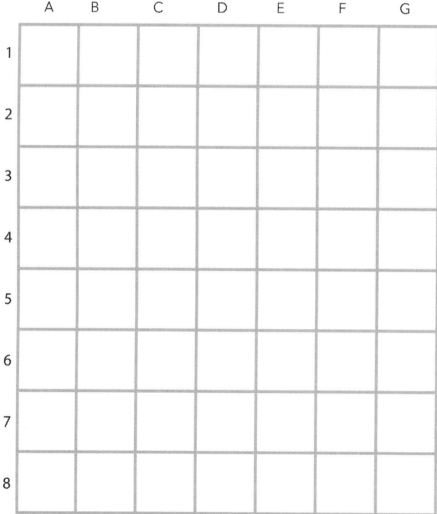

Can you draw this?

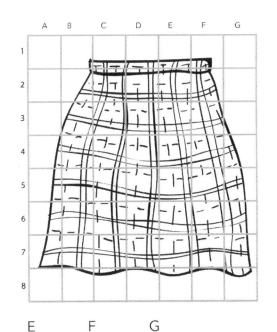

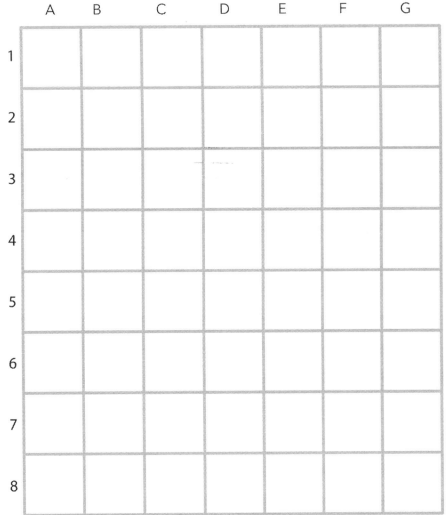

Can you draw this?

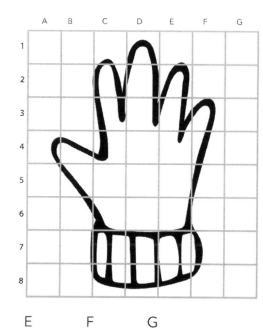

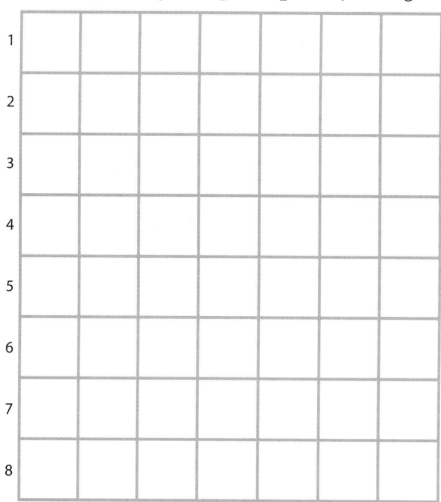

Can you draw this?

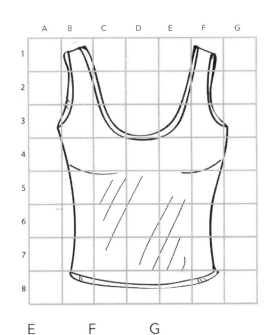

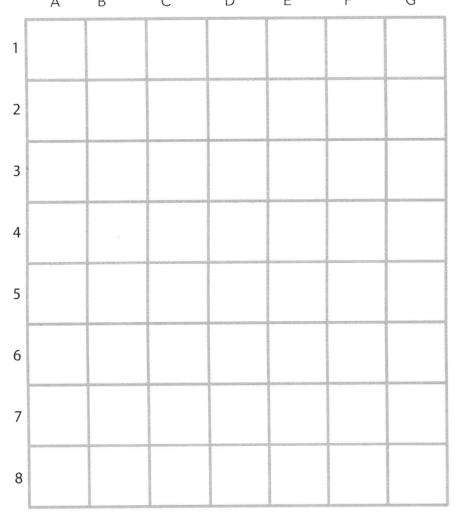

Can you draw this?

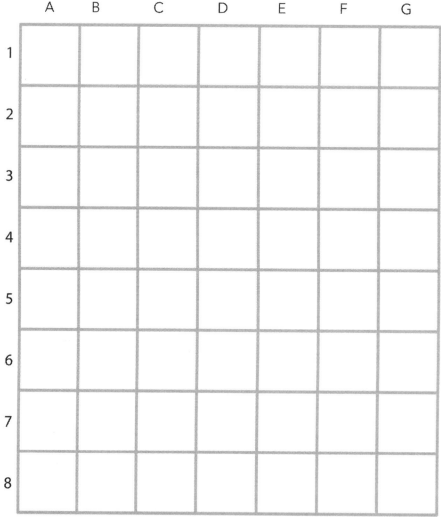

Can you draw this?

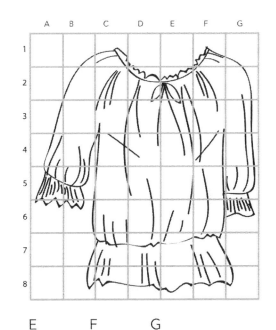

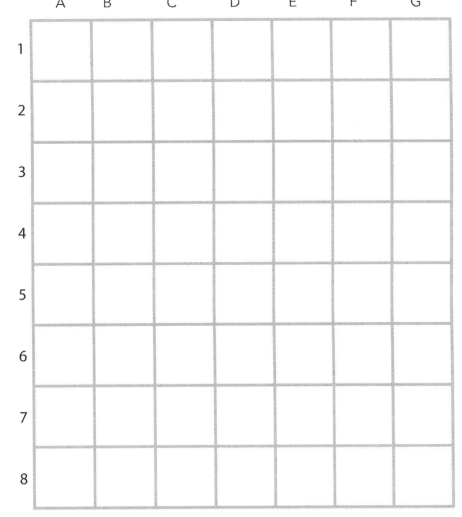

Can you draw this?

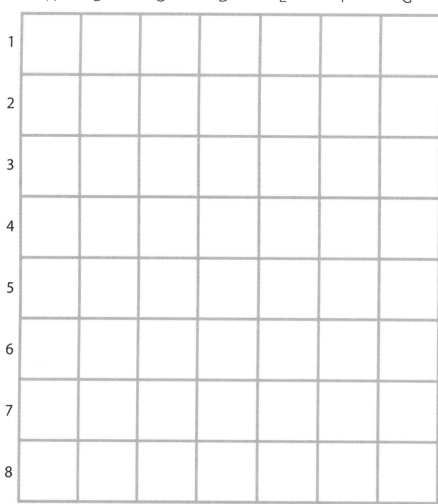

Can you draw this?

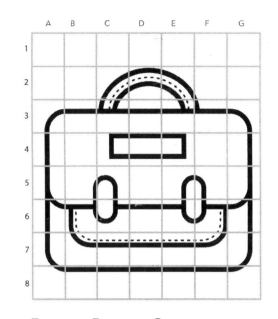

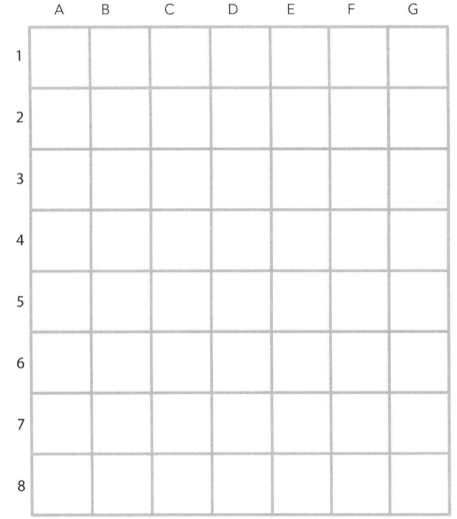

Can you draw this?

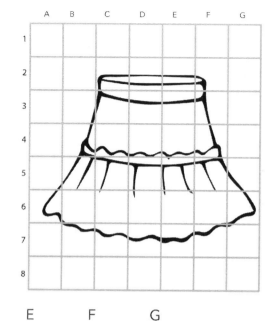

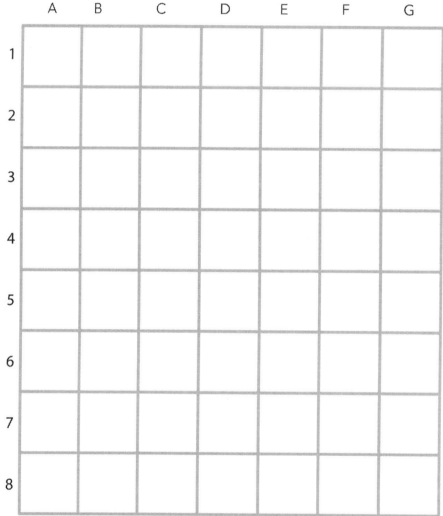

Can you draw this?

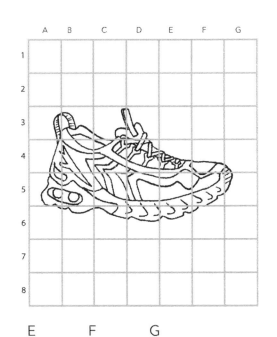

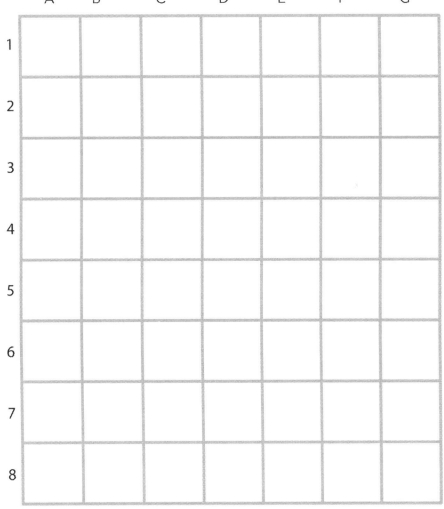

Can you draw this?

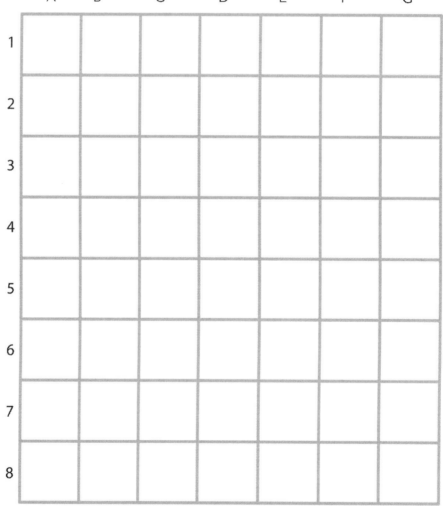

Can you draw this?

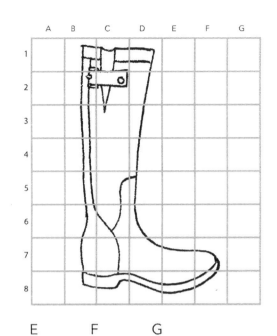

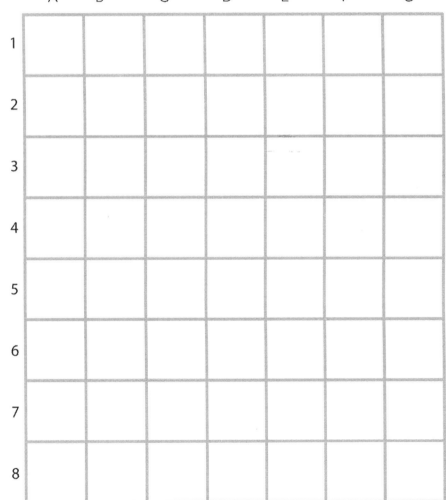

Can you draw this?

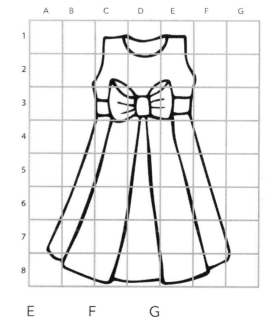

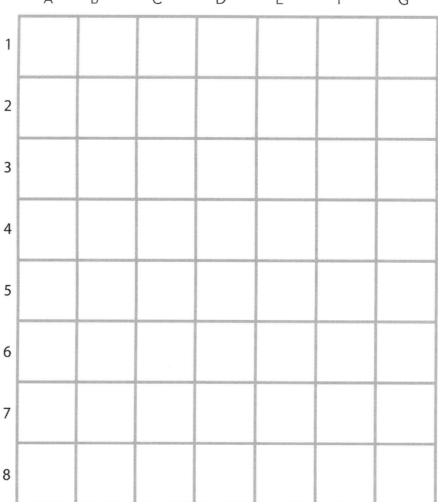

Can you draw this?

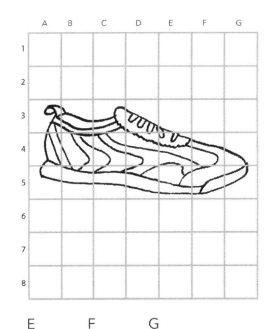

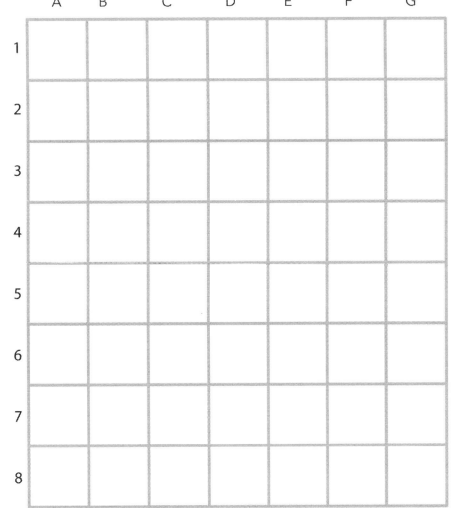

Can you draw this?

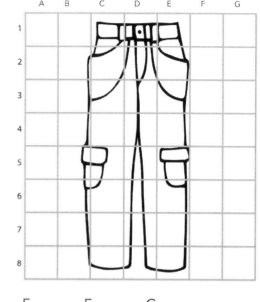

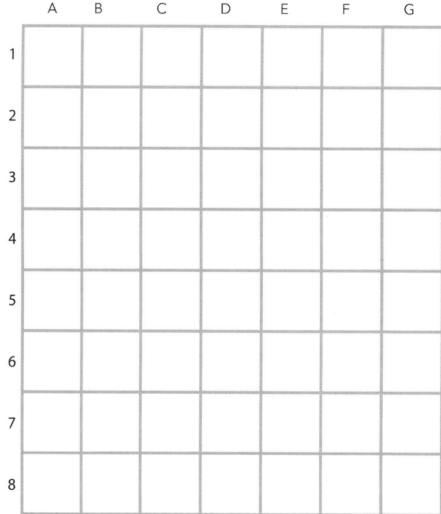

Can you draw this?

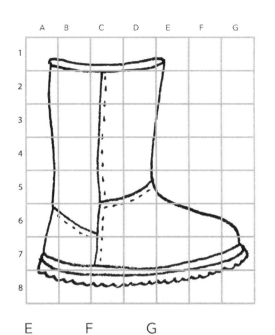

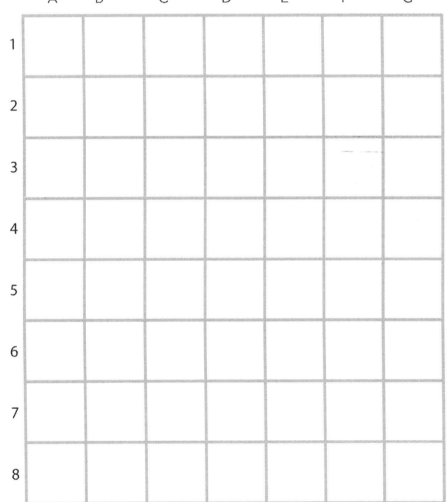

Can you draw this?

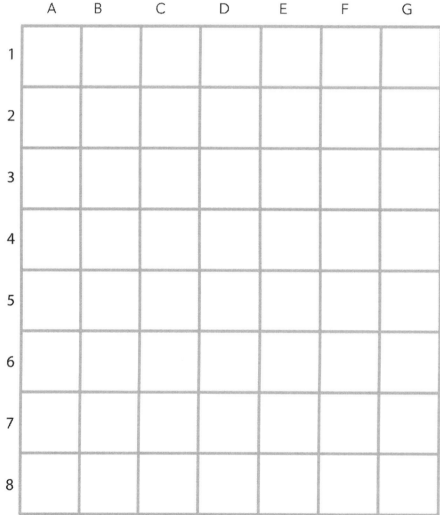

Can you draw this?

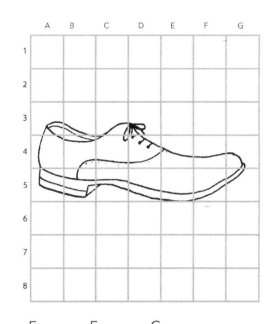

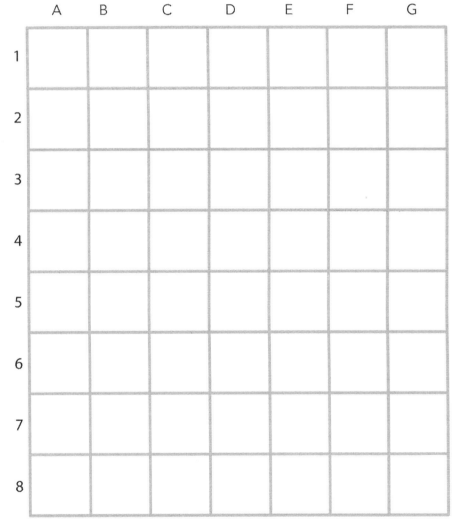

Can you draw this?

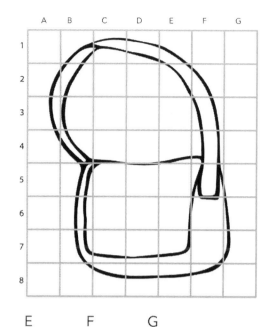

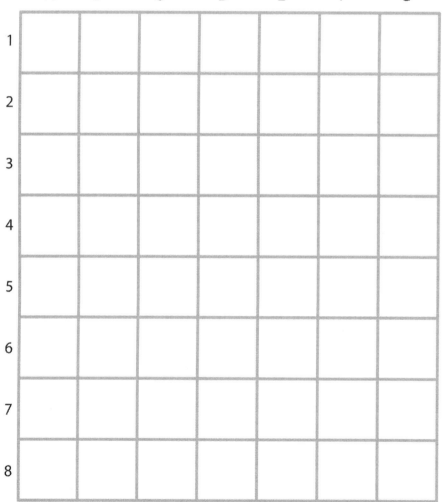

Can you draw this?

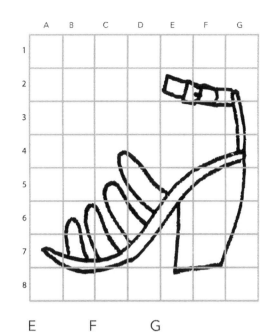

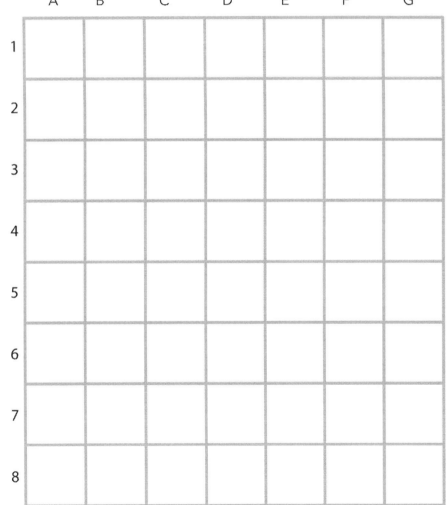

Can you draw this?

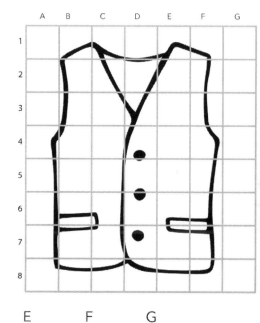

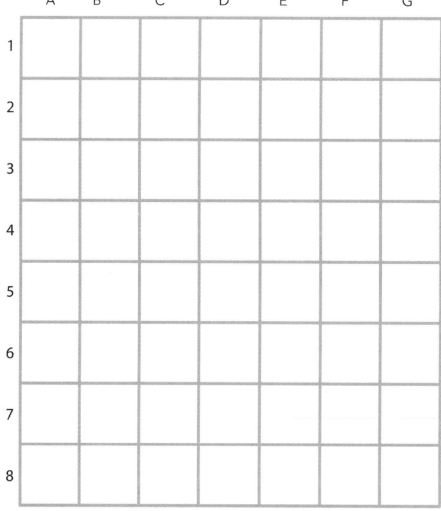

Can you draw this?

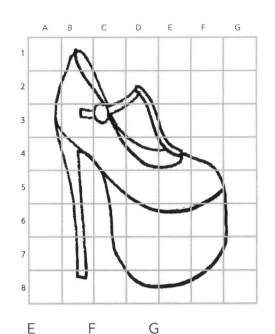

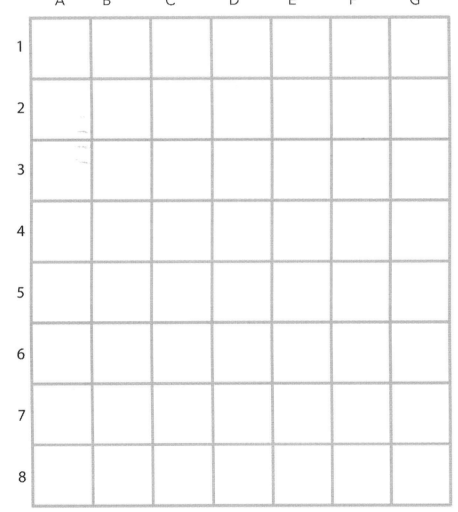

Can you draw this?

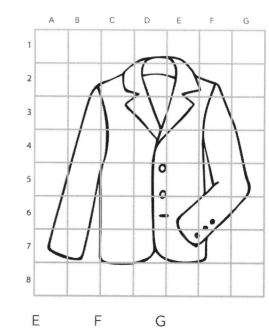

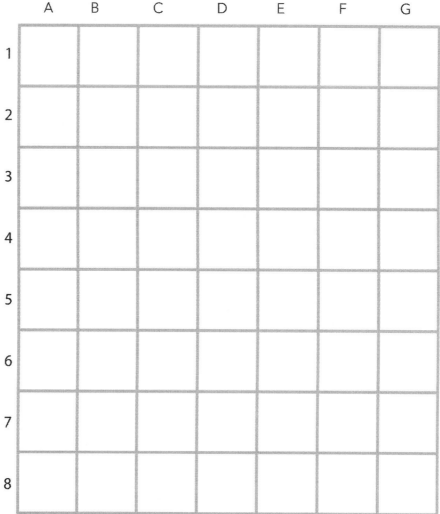

Can you draw this?

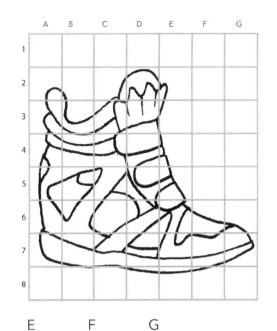

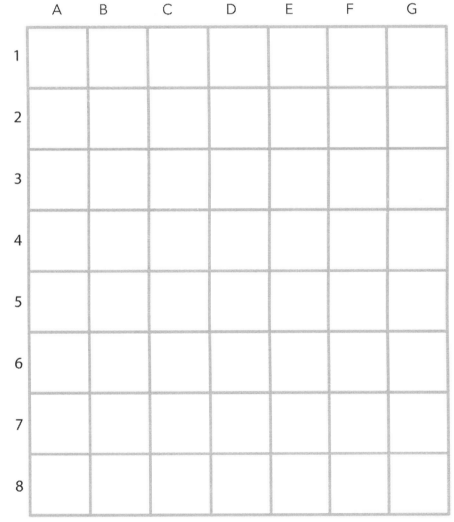

Can you draw this?

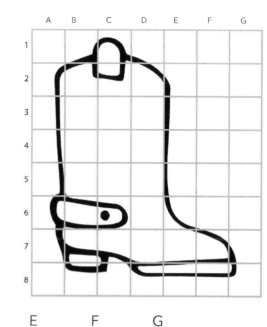

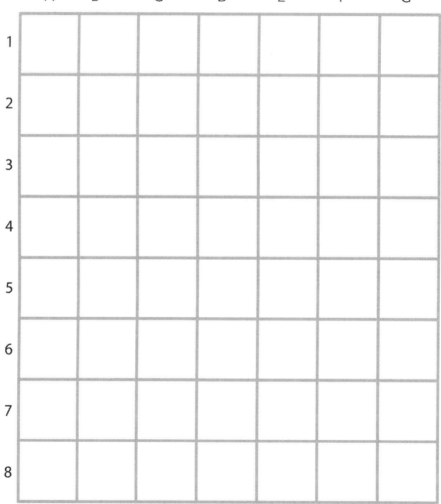

Can you draw this?

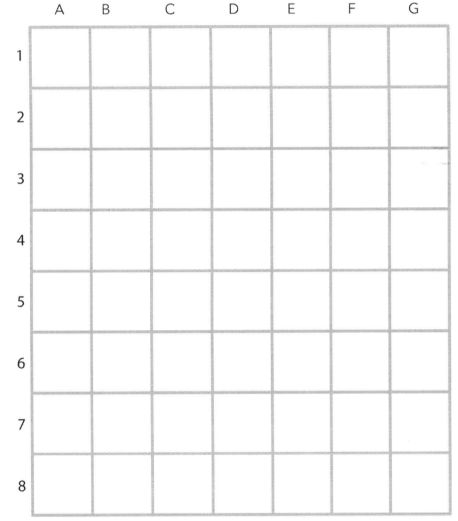

Can you draw this?

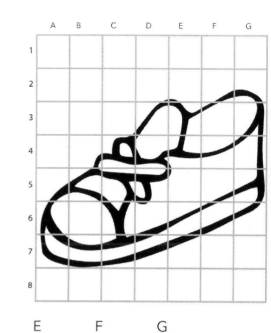

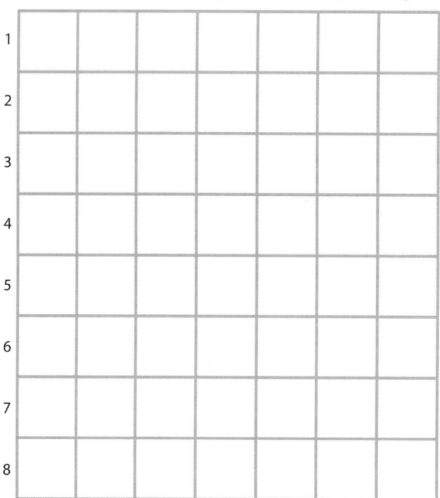

Can you draw this?

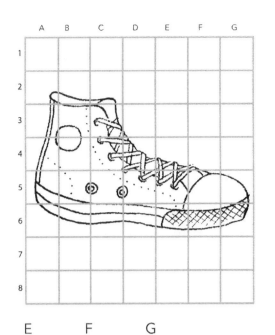

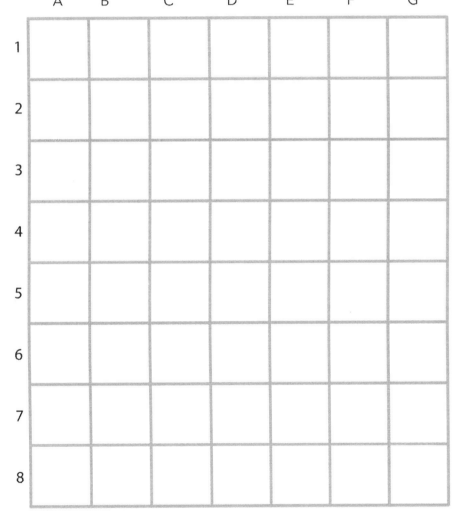

Can you draw this?

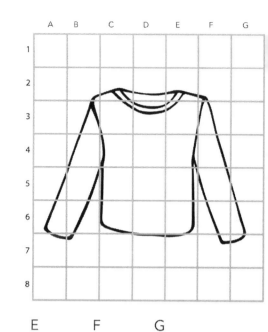

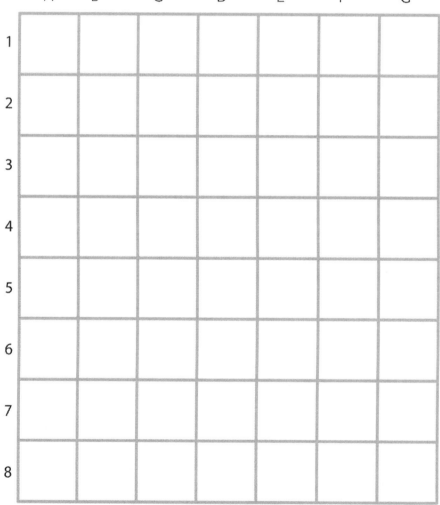

Can you draw this?

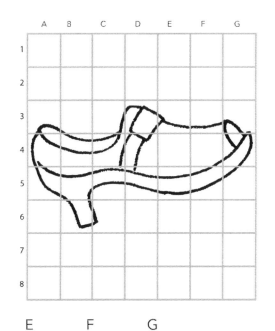

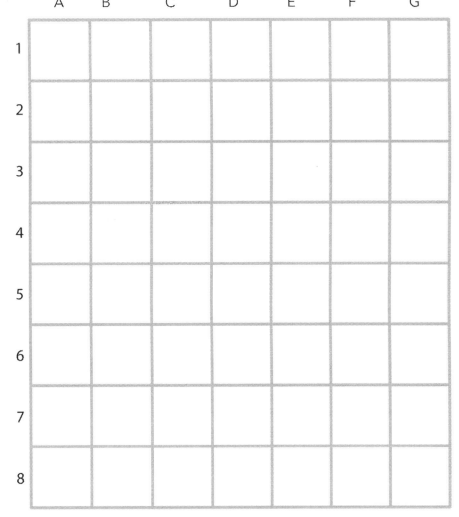

Can you draw this?

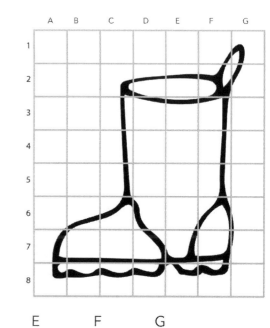

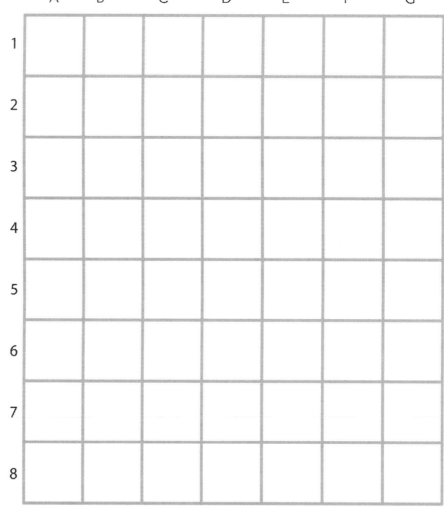

Can you draw this?

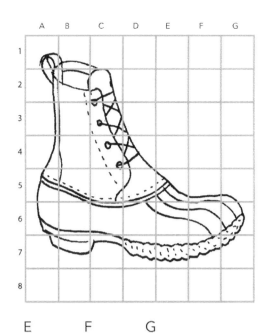

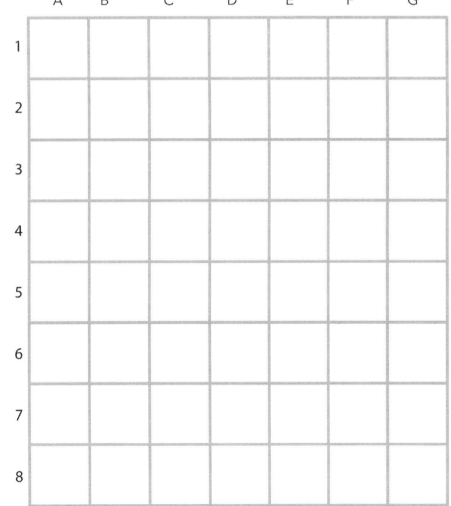

Can you draw this?

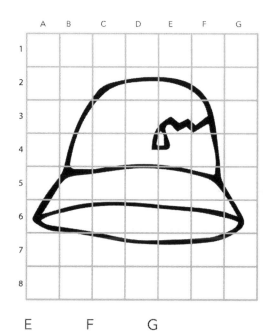

	A	B	C	D	E	F	G
1							
2							
3							
4							
5							
6							
7							
8							

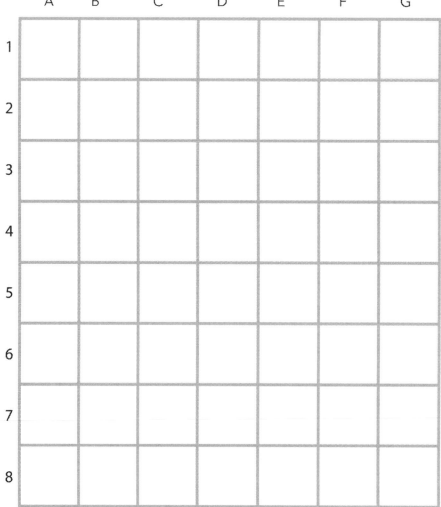

Can you draw this?

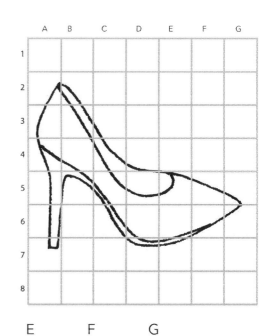

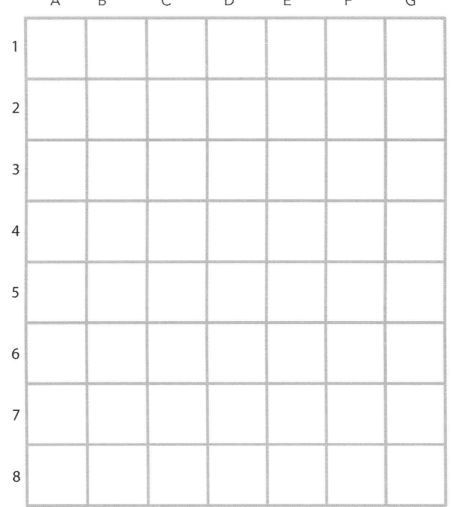

Can you draw this?

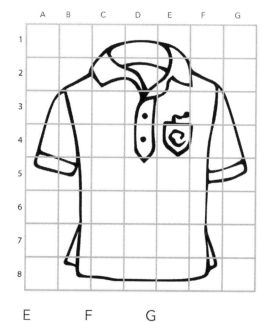

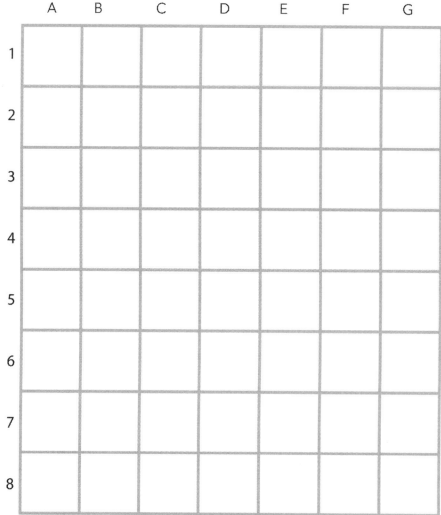

Can you draw this?

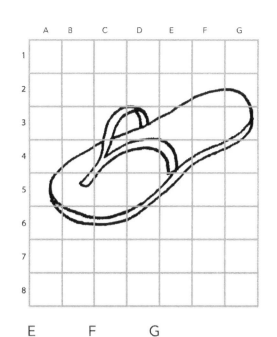

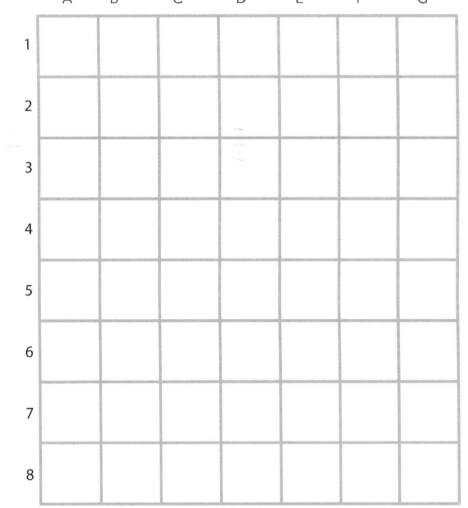

Can you draw this?

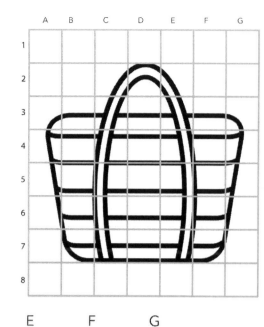

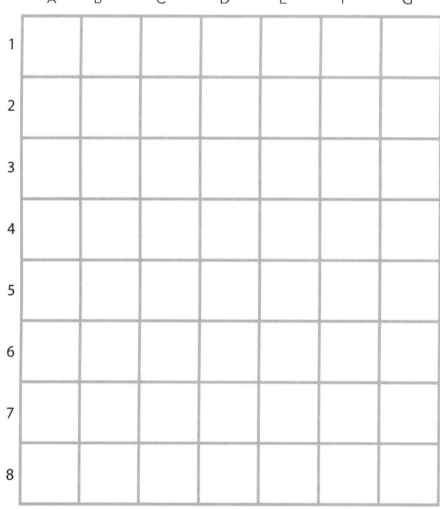

Can you draw this?

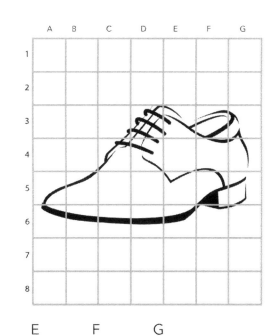

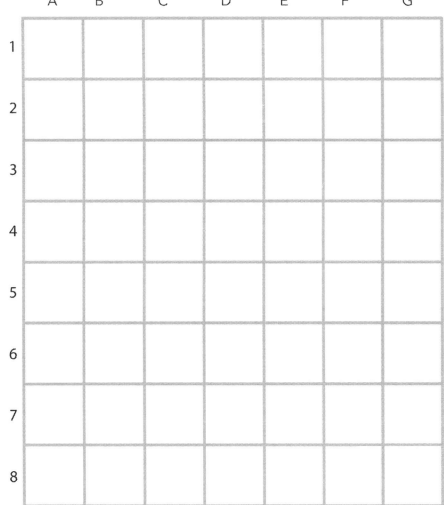

Can you draw this?

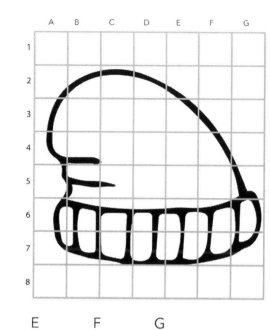

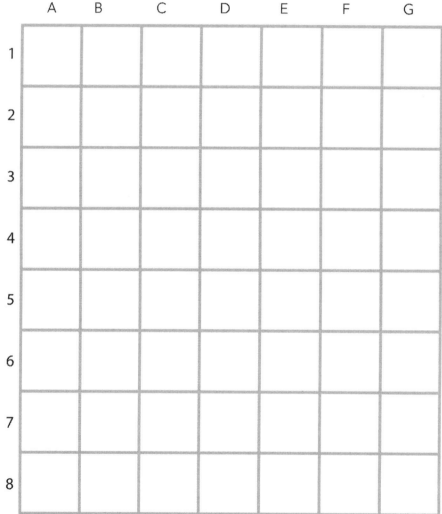

Can you draw this?

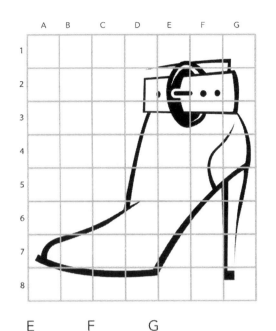

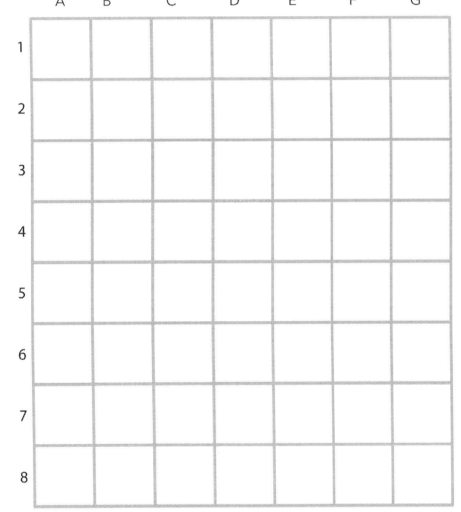

Can you draw this?

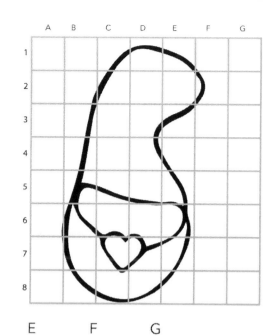

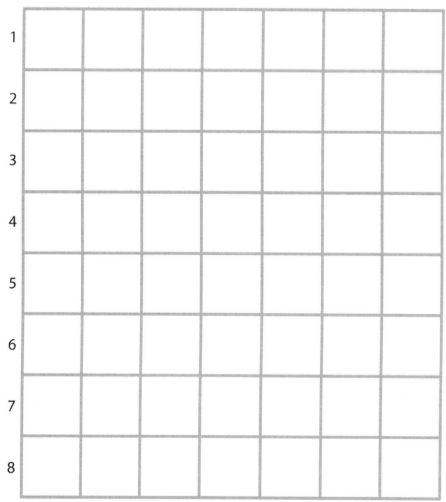

Can you draw this?

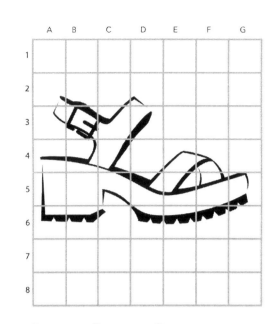

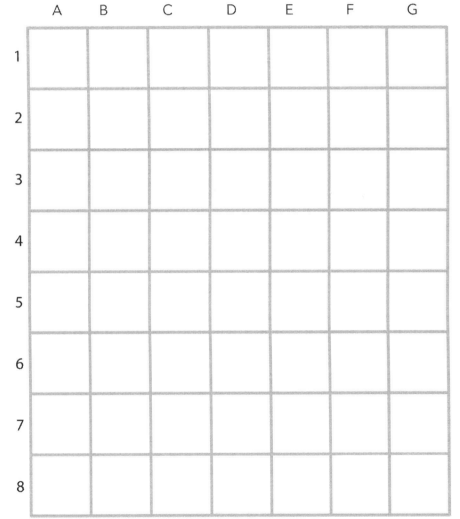

Can you draw this?

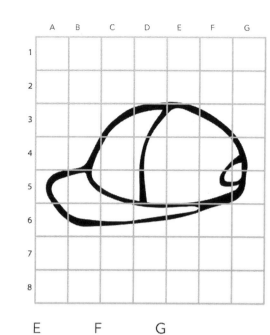

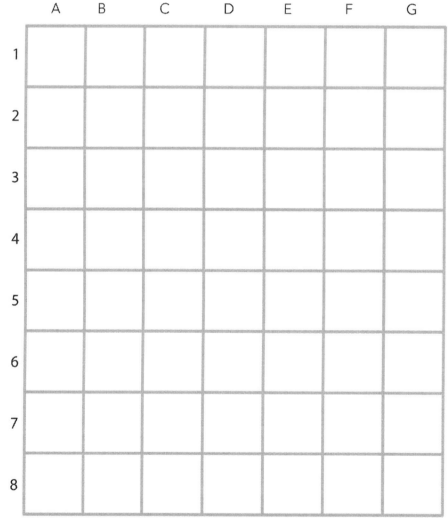

Can you draw this?

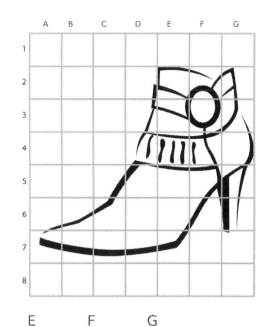

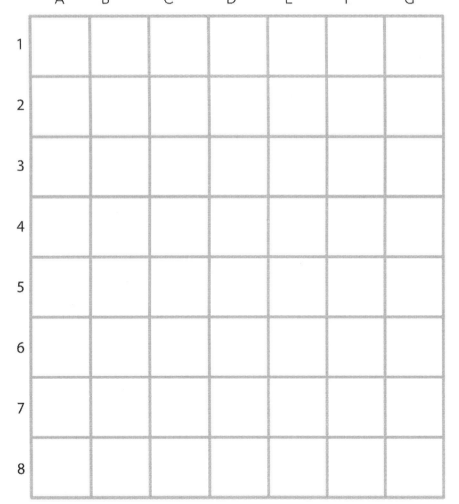

Can you draw this?

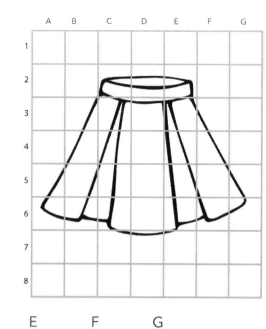

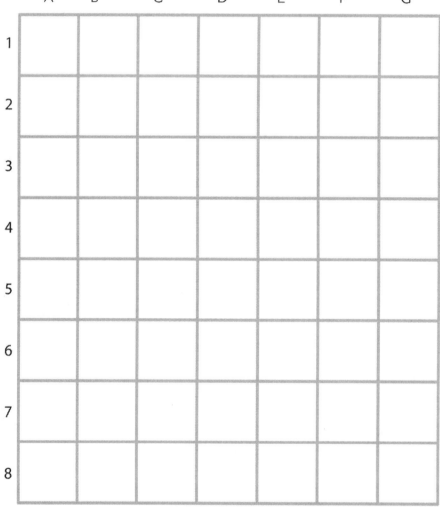

Can you draw this?

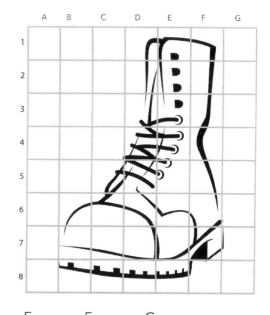

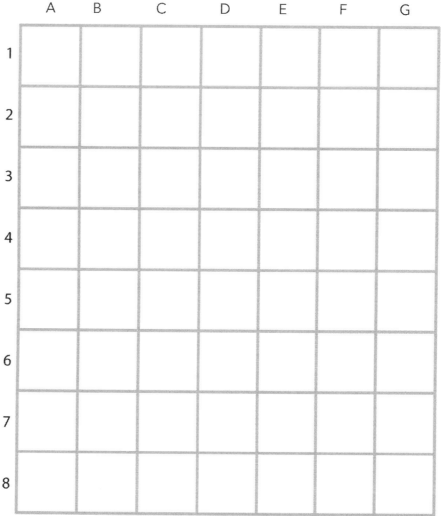

Can you draw this?

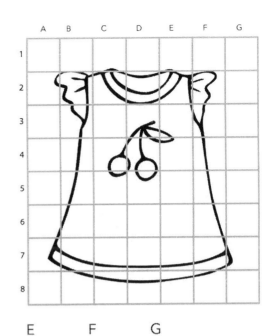

	A	B	C	D	E	F	G
1							
2							
3							
4							
5							
6							
7							
8							

Can you draw this?

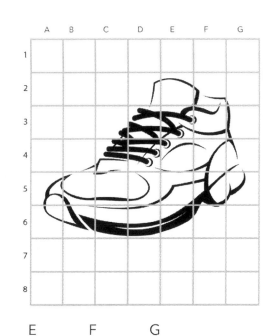

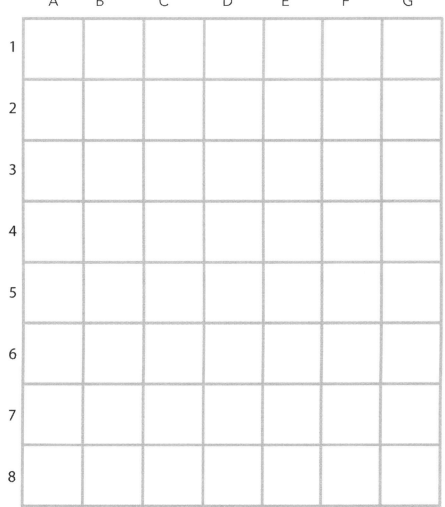

Can you draw this?

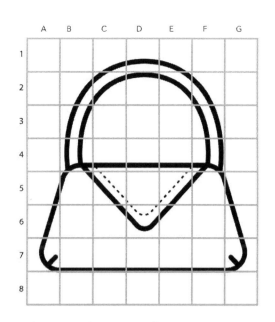

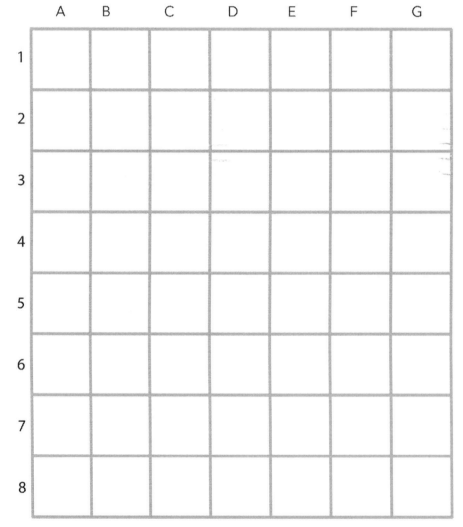

Can you draw this?

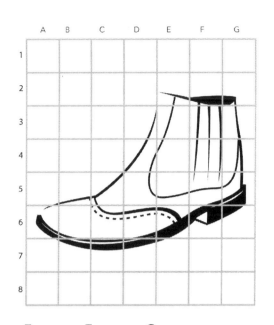

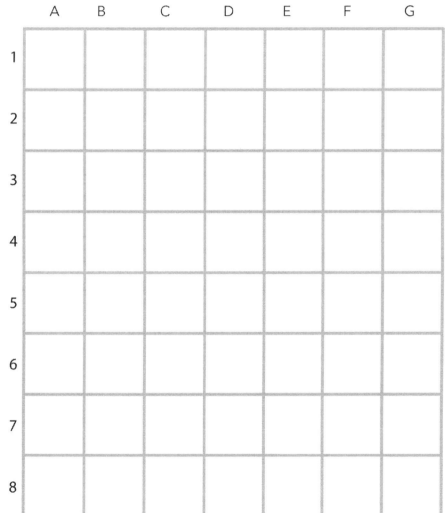

Can you draw this?

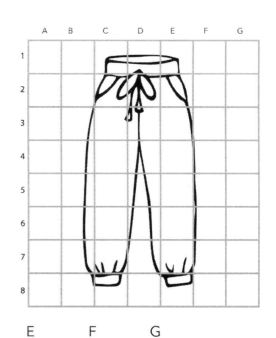

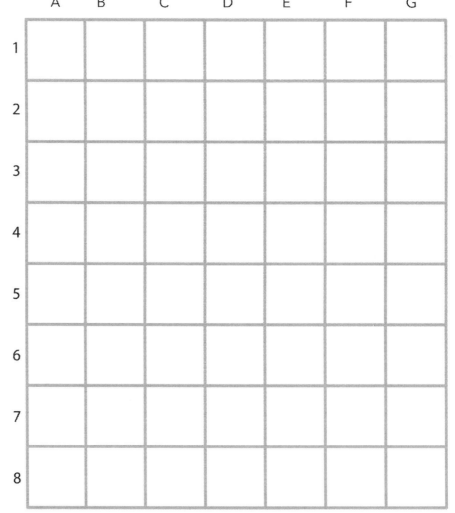

Can you draw this?

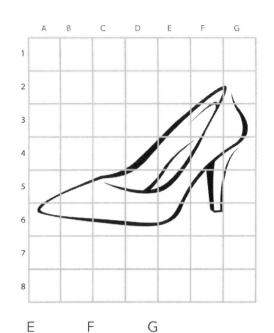

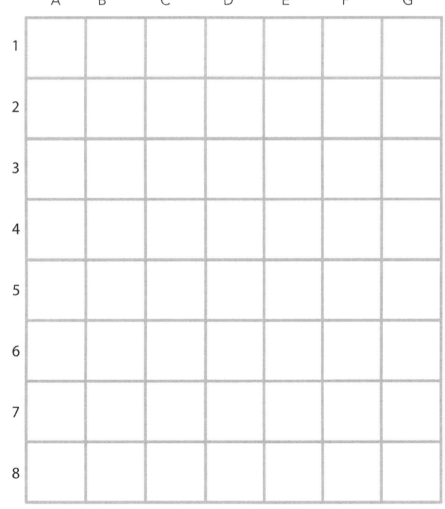

Can you draw this?

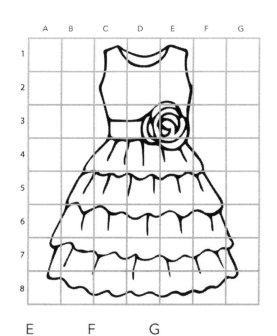

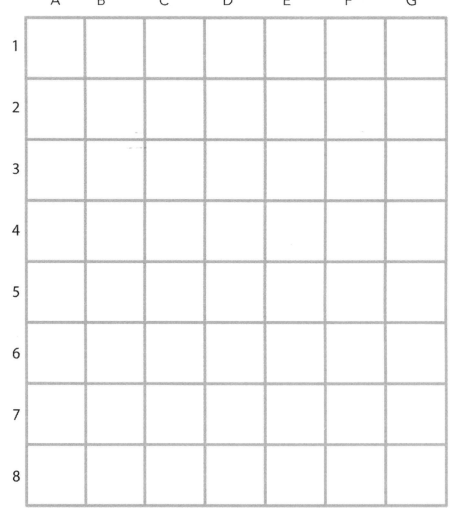

Can you draw this?

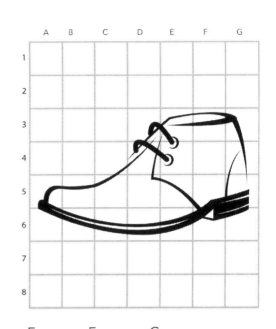

A B C D E F G

1
2
3
4
5
6
7
8

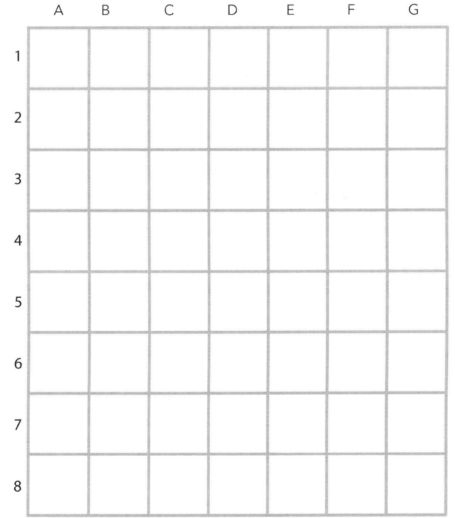

Can you draw this?

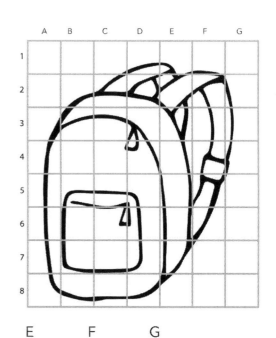

	A	B	C	D	E	F	G
1							
2							
3							
4							
5							
6							
7							
8							

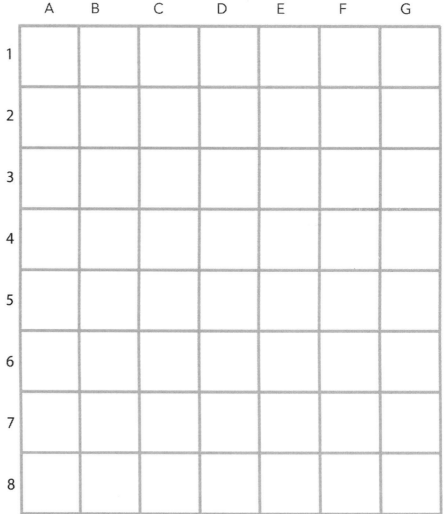

Can you draw this?

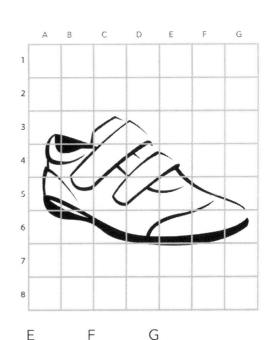

	A	B	C	D	E	F	G
1							
2							
3							
4							
5							
6							
7							
8							

Can you draw this?

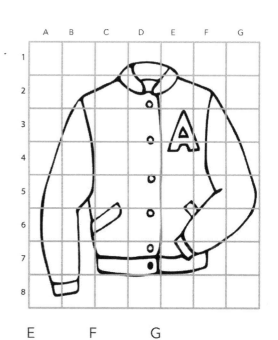

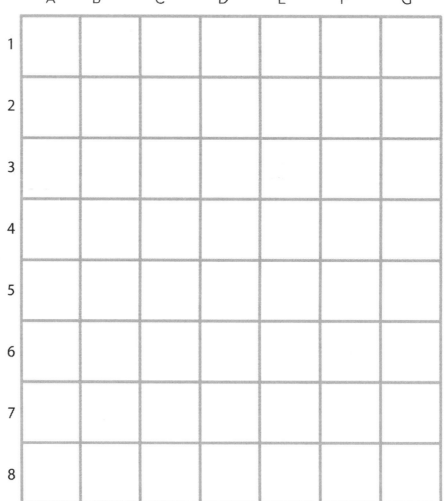

Can you draw this?

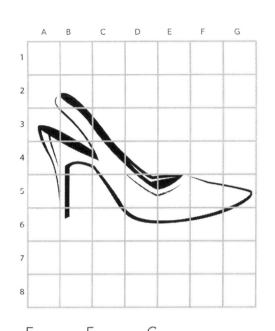

	A	B	C	D	E	F	G
1							
2							
3							
4							
5							
6							
7							
8							

Can you draw this?

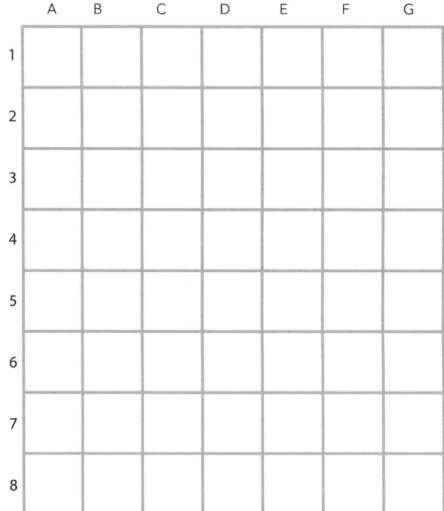

Can you draw this?

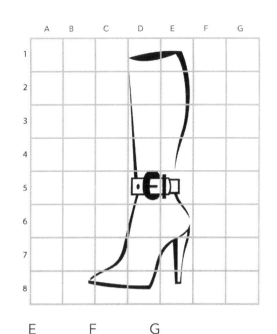

	A	B	C	D	E	F	G
1							
2							
3							
4							
5							
6							
7							
8							

Can you draw this?

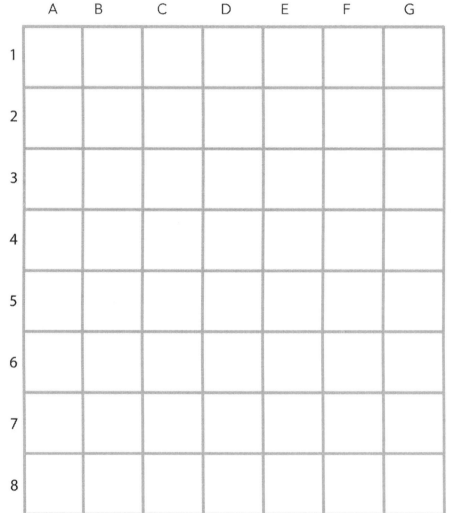

Can you draw this?

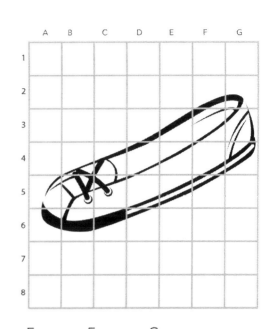

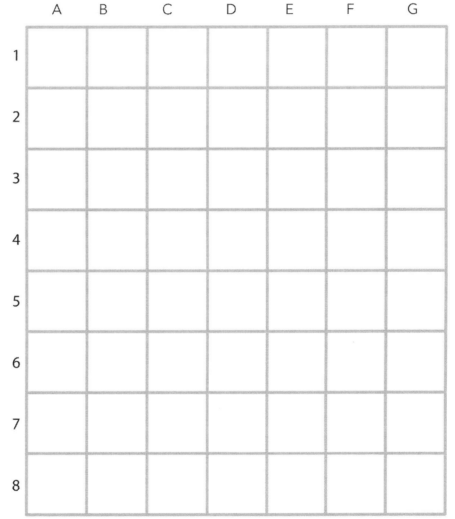

Can you draw this?

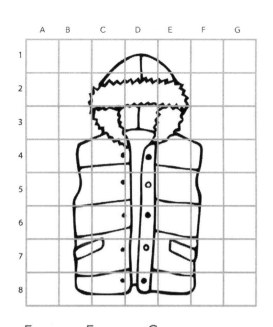

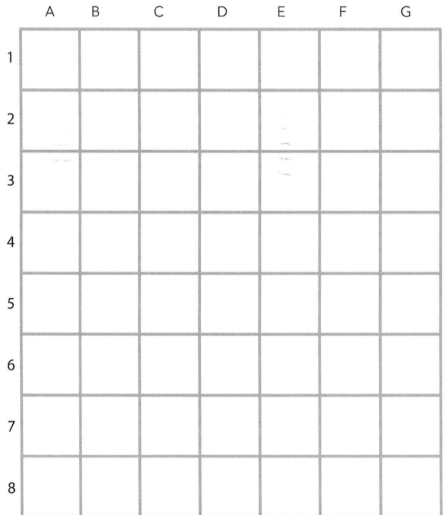

Can you draw this?

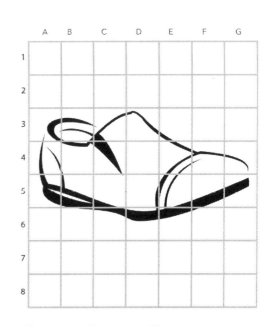

A B C D E F G

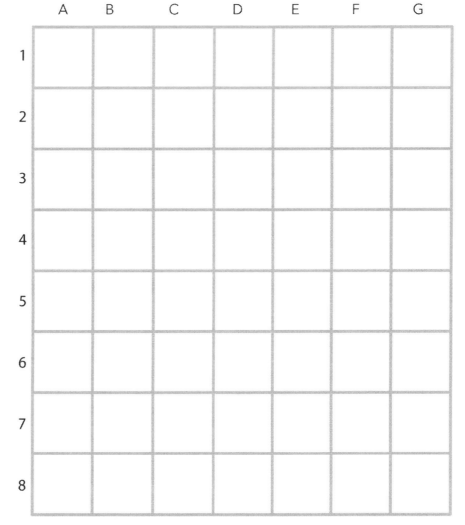

Can you draw this?

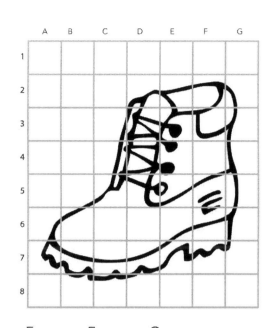

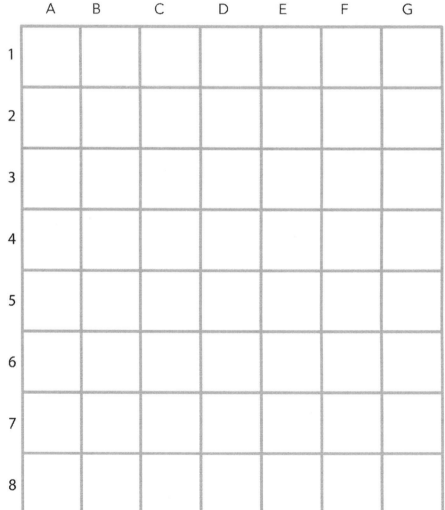

Can you draw this?

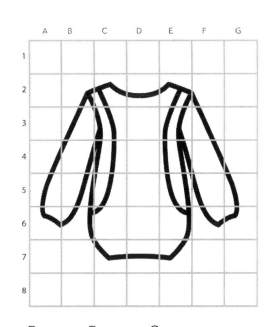

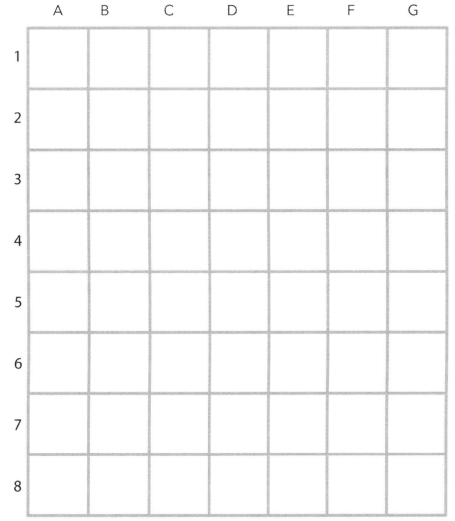

Can you draw this?

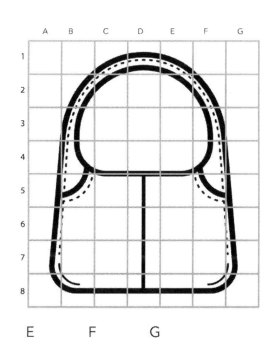

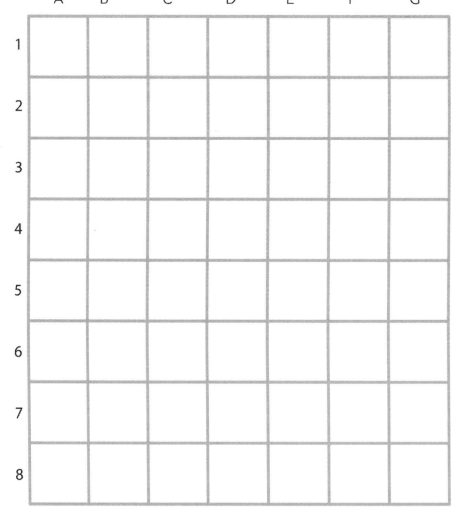

Can you draw this?

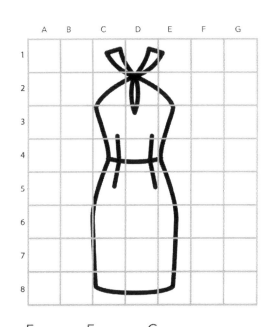

	A	B	C	D	E	F	G
1							
2							
3							
4							
5							
6							
7							
8							

Can you draw this?

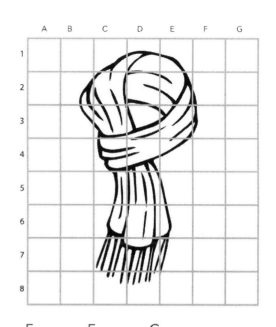

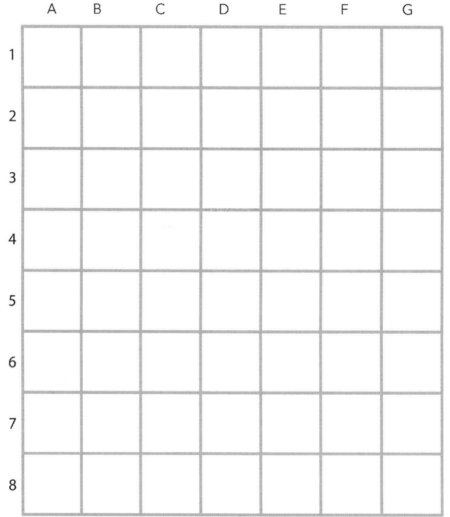

Can you draw this?

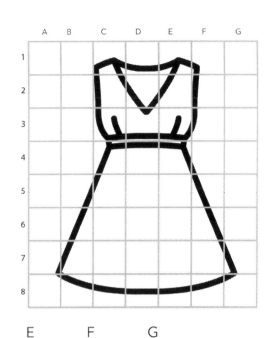

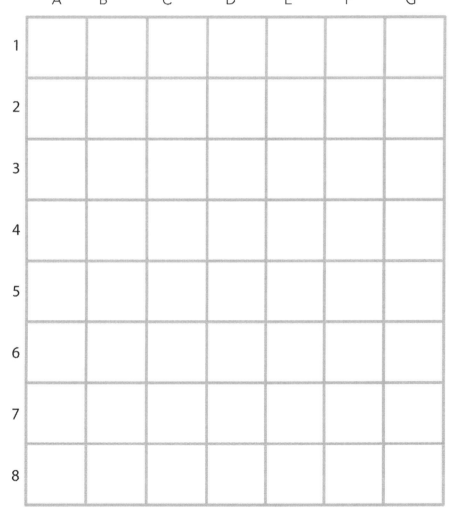

Can you draw this?

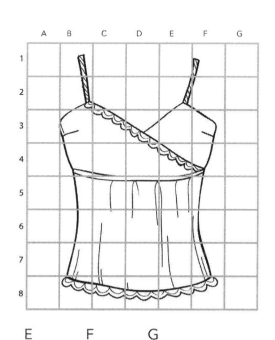

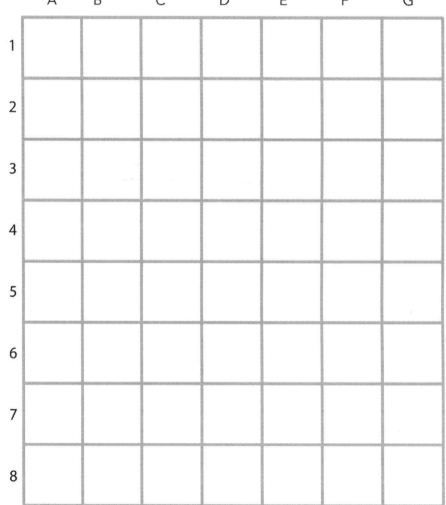

Can you draw this?

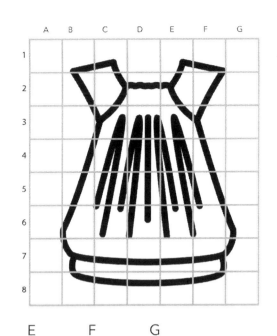

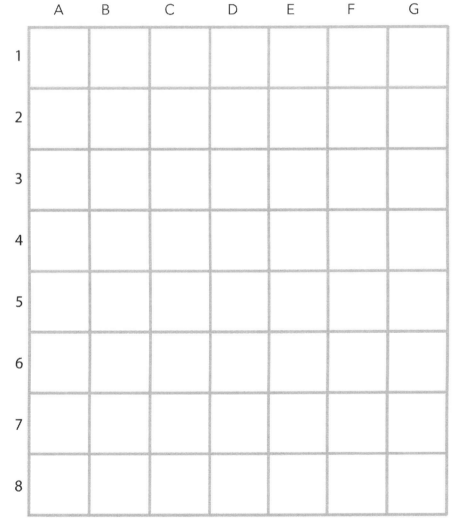

Can you draw this?

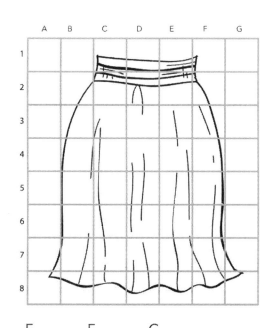

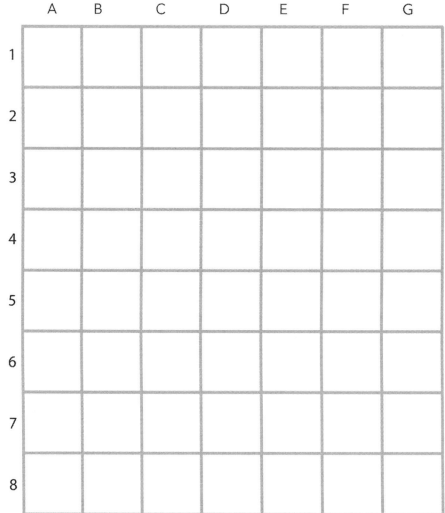

Can you draw this?

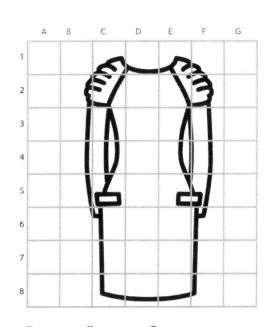

	A	B	C	D	E	F	G
1							
2							
3							
4							
5							
6							
7							
8							

Can you draw this?

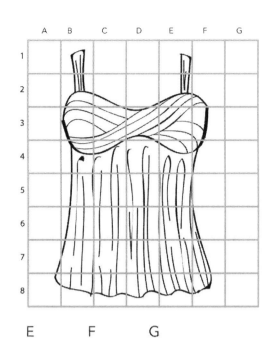

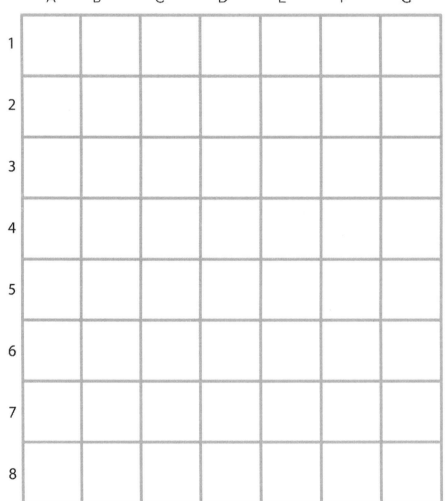

Can you draw this?

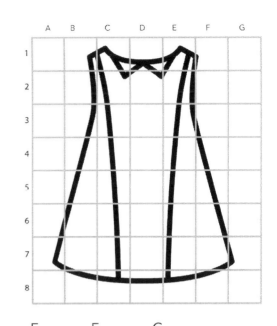

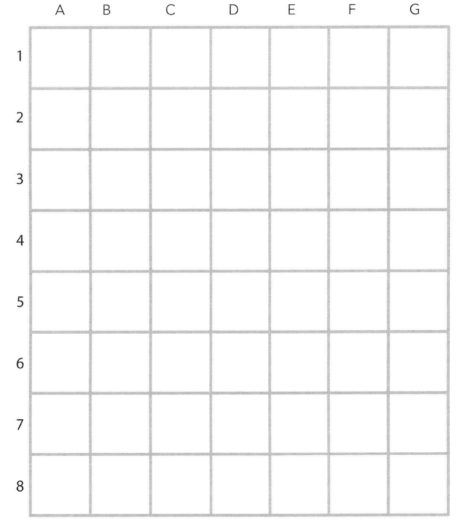

Can you draw this?

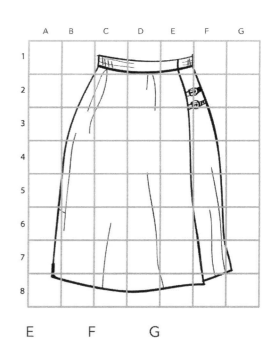

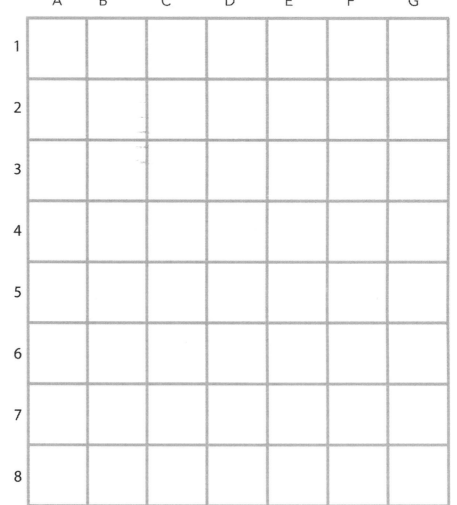

Can you draw this?

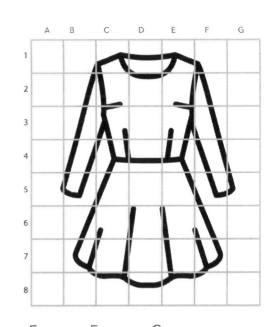

	A	B	C	D	E	F	G
1							
2							
3							
4							
5							
6							
7							
8							

Can you draw this?

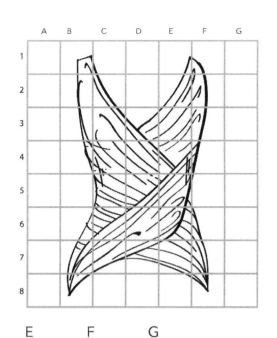

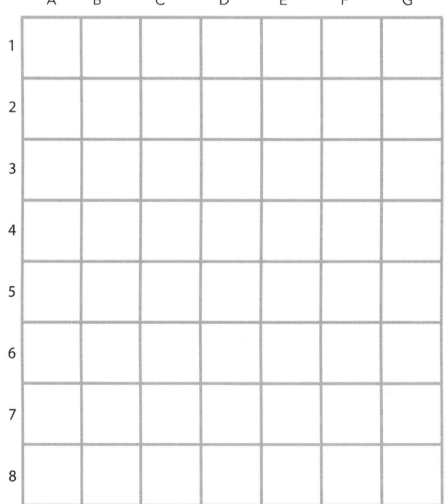

Can you draw this?

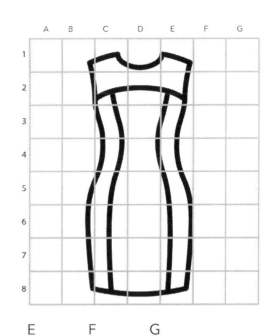

	A	B	C	D	E	F	G
1							
2							
3							
4							
5							
6							
7							
8							

Can you draw this?

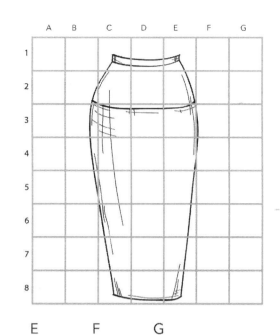

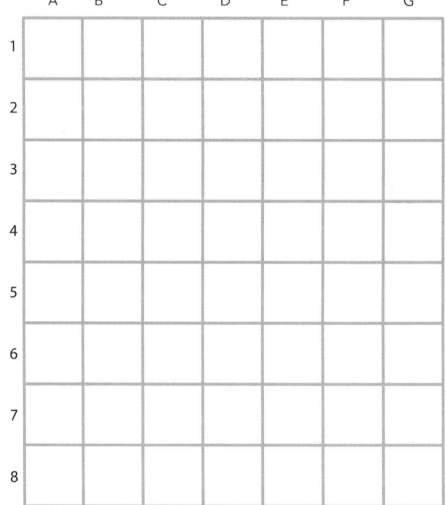

Can you draw this?

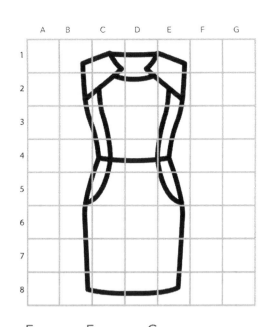

	A	B	C	D	E	F	G
1							
2							
3							
4							
5							
6							
7							
8							

Can you draw this?

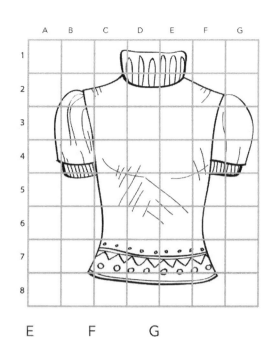

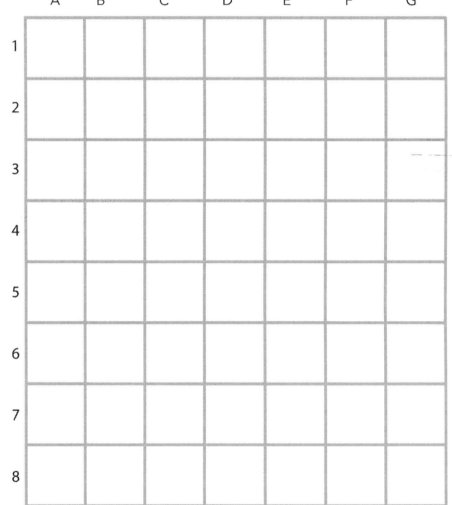

Can you draw this?

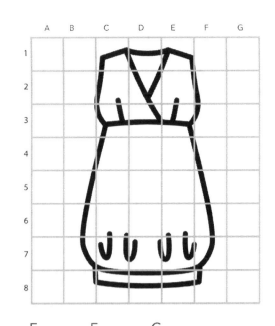

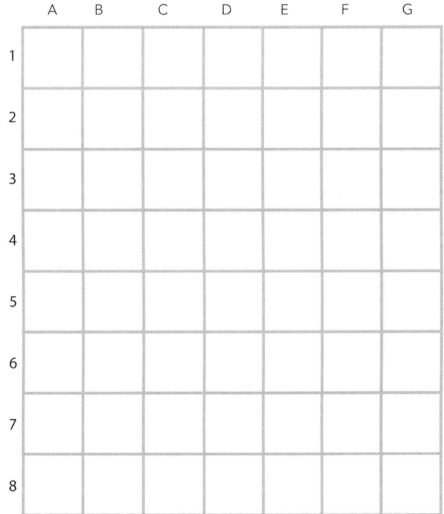

Can you draw this?

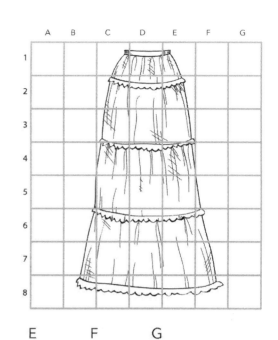

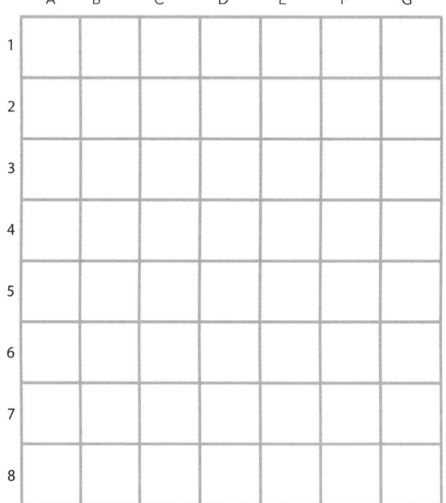

Can you draw this?

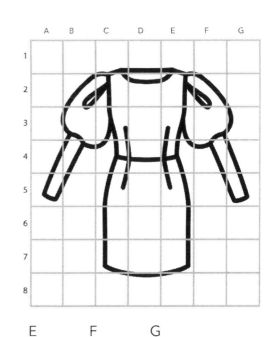

	A	B	C	D	E	F	G
1							
2							
3							
4							
5							
6							
7							
8							

Can you draw this?

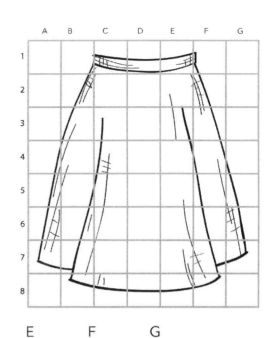

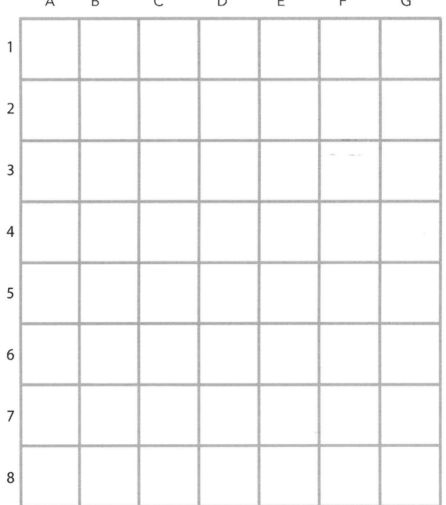

Can you draw this?

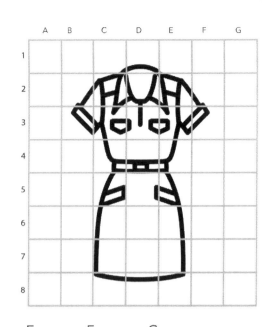

	A	B	C	D	E	F	G
1							
2							
3							
4							
5							
6							
7							
8							

Can you draw this?

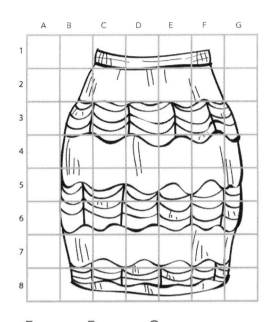

	A	B	C	D	E	F	G
1							
2							
3							
4							
5							
6							
7							
8							

Can you draw this?

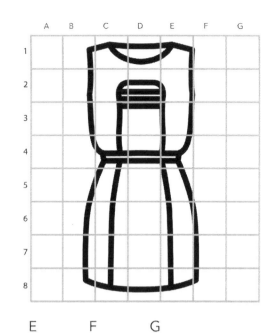

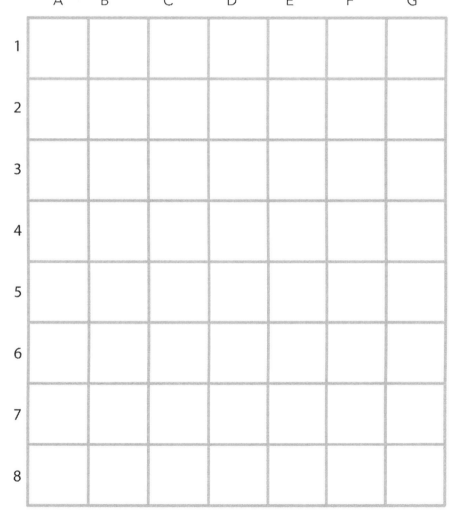

Can you draw this?

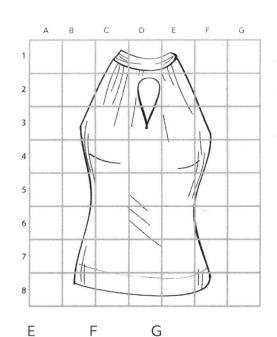

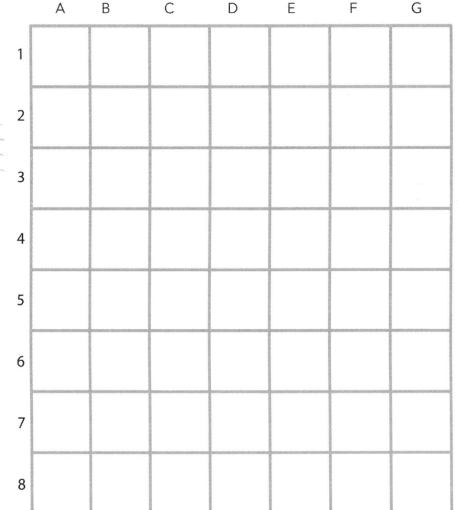

Can you draw this?

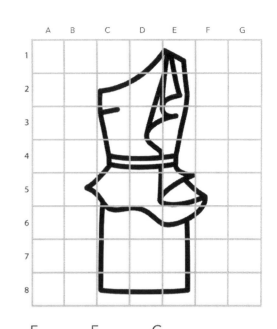

	A	B	C	D	E	F	G
1							
2							
3							
4							
5							
6							
7							
8							

Can you draw this?

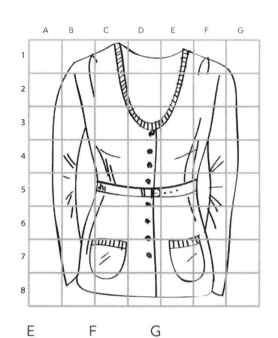

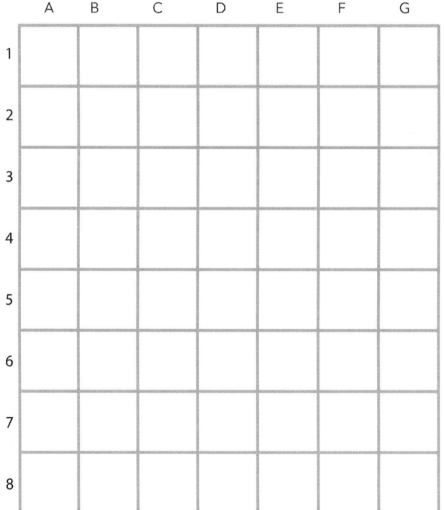

Can you draw this?

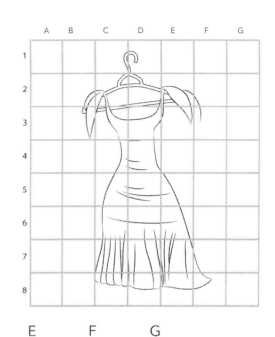

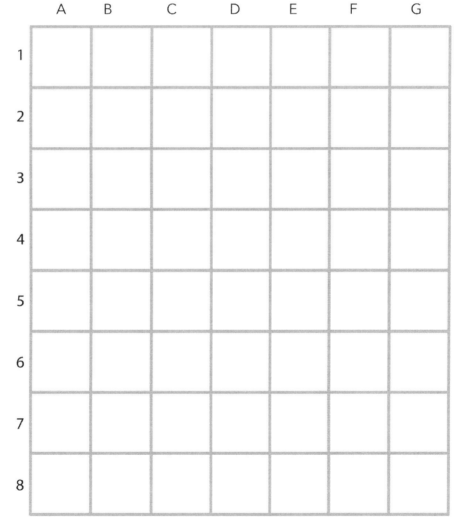

Can you draw this?

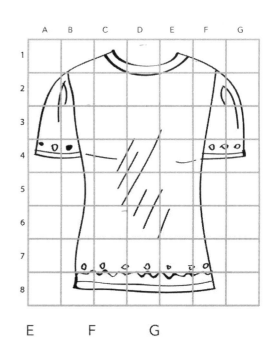

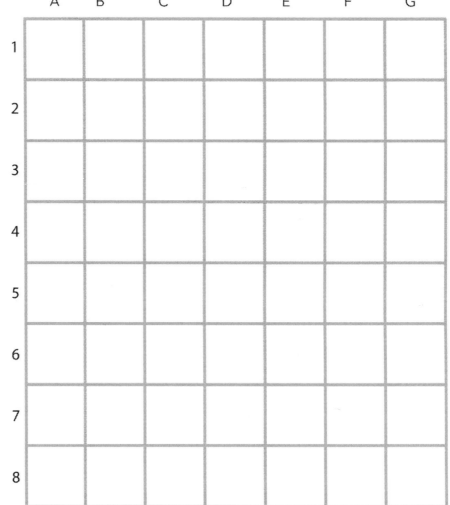

Can you draw this?

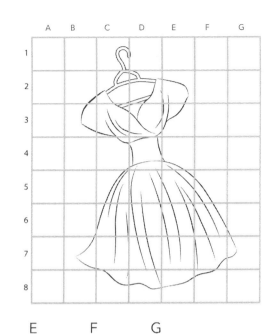

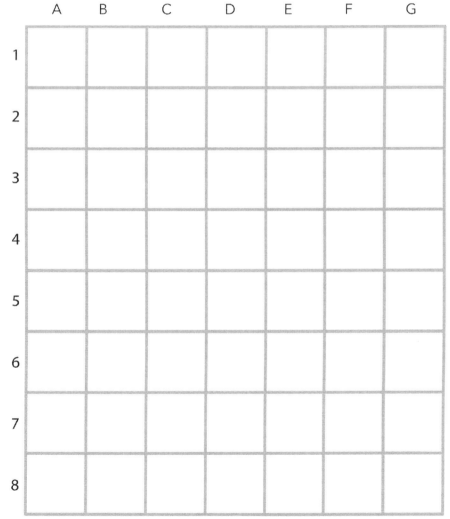

Made in the USA
San Bernardino, CA
18 July 2017